Hound Gelert
and
Wookey Witch

Creepy crawly caterpillar   page 3

Hound Gelert   page 5

Wookey Witch   page 19

Nelson

Thomas Nelson and Sons Ltd
Nelson House   Mayfield Road
Walton-on-Thames   Surrey
KT12 5PL   UK

51 York Place
Edinburgh
EH1 3JD   UK

Thomas Nelson (Hong Kong) Ltd
Toppan Building 10/F
22A Westlands Road
Quarry Bay   Hong Kong

Thomas Nelson Australia
102 Dodds Street
South Melbourne
Victoria 3205   Australia

Nelson Canada
1120 Birchmount Road
Scarborough Ontario
M1K 5G4   Canada

© Macmillan Education Ltd 1987
This edition © Thomas Nelson & Sons Ltd 1992
Editorial Consultant: Donna Bailey
'Creepy crawly caterpillar' was written by Peggy Clulow and illustrated by Joyce
Smith and David Dowland
'Hound Gelert' was written by Kath Davies and illustrated by Shirley Tourret
'Wookey Witch' was written by Jean Chapman and illustrated by Derek Collard

First published by Macmillan Education Ltd 1987
ISBN 0-333-41893-X

This edition published by Thomas Nelson and Sons Ltd 1992

ISBN 0-17-400619-5
NPN 9 8 7 6 5

All rights reserved. No paragraph of this publication may be reproduced, copied
or transmitted save with written permission or in accordance with the provisions
of the Copyright, Design and Patents Act 1988, or under the terms of any
licence permitting limited copying issued by the Copyright Licensing Agency,
90 Tottenham Court Road, London W1P 9HE.

Any person who does any unauthorised act in relation to this publication may be
liable to criminal prosecution and civil claims for damages.

Printed in Hong Kong

Creepy crawly caterpillar

Creepy crawly caterpillar,
Come and play with me.
It's time to stop your munching,
You've had breakfast, lunch and tea.

Creepy crawly caterpillar,
If you eat much more,
Your skin won't go on stretching
And you'll burst it, that's for sure.

Creepy crawly caterpillar
Looked at me and said,
"I burst my skin quite often
Till I'm well and truly fed."

Creepy crawly caterpillar
Gave a little smile,
"I don't think that you'll know me
In a very little while."

Creepy crawly caterpillar
Crept beneath a leaf;
He twisted and he wriggled,
It was quite beyond belief!

Creepy crawly caterpillar
Changed his shape that day;
His skin went hard as leather,
And he didn't want to play.

Creepy crawly caterpillar,
What's become of you?
You hang there without moving,
Won't you answer me? Please do.

Creepy crawly caterpillar
Stayed there many days.
I went to see him sometimes,
But he didn't change his ways.

Creepy crawly caterpillar
Burst his leather skin,
And something very different
Was just waiting there within.

Creepy crawly caterpillar
Spread his wings to dry;
Oh, crawly caterpillar,
You're a gorgeous butterfly.

4

Hound Gelert

Many, many years ago, in fact more than
eight hundred years ago, Prince Llewelyn lived
in his kingdom in Wales.

Wales was a wild country then. There were
wolves in the hills and wild stags and boars.
Prince Llewelyn loved to go hunting with his friends
every summer. They hunted the wild boar in the woods
and their dogs chased after them.

The Prince's favourite dog was a hound called Gelert.
He was brave and faithful and loyal and he never left
the Prince's side.

The Prince's family sometimes came with him on these summer visits. One year there was a special reason why the Prince did not want to leave them behind in his castle.

The Prince and Princess had a baby boy. They thought he was the most wonderful baby in the whole world. He lay in his cradle and he laughed and waved his tiny fists at everyone and made them smile too.

So the Princess and the baby and all the people of the court came with Prince Llewelyn on his visit that summer.

Now the Princess loved hunting almost as much as
Llewelyn did and she wanted to go out and chase
the wild boar with him.

They decided that the baby would be quite safe
in his cradle in the house. There were plenty of
people to look after him and Llewelyn said that
he would leave his faithful hound Gelert to guard
the baby as well.

The Prince always took Gelert hunting with him,
so Gelert was very surprised when he was told
to stay beside the baby's cradle.
He looked up at his master with a puzzled face as
Llewelyn told him to guard the baby with his life.
Gelert knew all about guarding Llewelyn.
He had saved the Prince's life when wild animals
had attacked him.
But who would want to harm a baby?

However, if that was what Llewelyn wanted him to do,
that was what Gelert would do. He stood beside
the baby's cradle as the hunting party set off.
Soon they were out of sight among the trees.

For a time Gelert could hear the sound of the
hunting-horn over the hills. It became fainter and
fainter until it died away completely. Only the sound
of the river rushing over the stones and the bees
buzzing in the sunshine disturbed the silence
of the sleepy valley. The baby was asleep and so was
his nurse. Only Gelert stayed awake, on guard.

High up in the woods, the hunt was becoming exciting. The Prince and his friends were chasing the biggest boar they had ever seen. It was a very clever beast and it kept getting away from them, just when they thought that the next spear or arrow would reach it.

Llewelyn had often heard about this boar from the people who lived in the woods. They were all afraid of it. But Llewelyn had never seen it before, although he had often searched for it. Now he had seen the boar, he did not want to lose it. He followed it on and on, going deeper and deeper into the woods.

Suddenly Llewelyn saw that the sun had gone behind the hills. Soon it would be dark, and they were a long way from home.

The Prince called his friends, and the hunting-horn rang out over the darkening woods. The hounds stopped chasing the great boar, and everyone turned back the way they had come. As they did so, they heard a faraway sound which made them shiver.
It was the cry of wolves, howling in the hills.

It was a long ride back, and it was almost dark
when the Prince and Princess arrived at the house.
They were tired and hungry and very anxious
to see their baby son.

"Gelert will be glad to see us too," said the Prince.
"I'm sure we would have caught that boar if
he had been with us. He is by far the bravest
of all my hounds."

"But we had to leave him behind," said the Princess.
"We had to leave him to guard the baby."

Everything was very quiet in the house.
They got down from their horses. Where were
all the people? Why was there no one to meet them?

The Prince and Princess went straight to the room
where they had left the baby.

They could not believe what they saw.
Stools and tables lay on their sides.
There were broken pots all over the floor and
even the baby's cradle was upside down.
There was no sign of anyone.

Gelert, who was lying in a corner, jumped up
and ran over to his master, wagging his tail.
Llewelyn was horrified. He saw that the room
was covered in blood and there was blood
on Gelert too.

At once Llewelyn thought he knew what must have happened. He knew that dogs sometimes went mad and attacked their owners. Now he thought that Gelert had gone mad too and had killed the baby.

Before anyone could stop him, the Prince pulled out his sword and killed Gelert. Then Llewelyn and the Princess wept, because they thought their baby was dead.

Suddenly they heard a tiny cry. It came from
the up-turned cradle. They rushed to it and
lifted it up.

And there, quite safe, lay their baby son.
He smiled and laughed and waved his tiny fists in
the air at them. And near the baby, half-hidden by
a pile of rugs, was the body of a great grey wolf.

With a shout, Llewelyn picked up the baby and
hugged him. It was the Princess who realised
the truth about what had happened.

"Oh, Llewelyn!" she cried. "Gelert was faithful
after all. Look, he has killed the wolf and
saved our son. Everyone else has run away!"

Then Llewelyn knew that Gelert had been brave and
loyal to the end. He had fought the wolf and killed it
to protect the baby. The blood was the wolf's blood,
not the baby's. And he, Llewelyn, had killed his most
faithful companion.

Then Llewelyn wept for Gelert too.
He took the body of his faithful friend and buried it
nearby, beside the river. He told everyone that he had
been wrong about Gelert and had killed him by mistake.
He told everyone how brave Gelert was, and how he had
saved the baby's life.

The people told Llewelyn that they had been so
frightened when the big grey wolf came that they had
all run away. Only Gelert had stayed.
He would not leave the baby.

A village grew up beside the river in the valley.
It is still there today. It is called 'Beddgelert',
which means 'Gelert's Grave'.

There is also a stone set in the field near
the river, and on it is carved the story of Gelert.
The stone was put there many years after Gelert died,
so that no one will ever forget the story of
the brave hound Gelert.

Wookey Witch

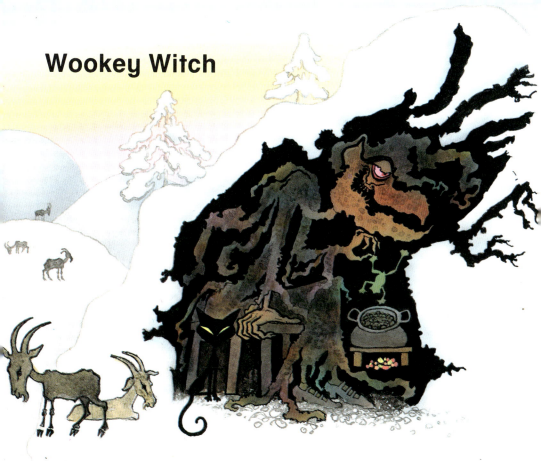

    Long ago, an old woman, her cat and her goats lived
in a cave on a hill. She was a bad one, a wild one.
She was the Witch of Wookey Hill.

    At the foot of the hill was a village, but all
was not well there. The winter had gone on and on.
There seemed to be no end to it. The wind blew and
blew and the snow was heavy on the fields and
the roads. It almost hid the village huts, and
the river was frozen over with ice.

"The Witch has put a spell on us," cried the people in the village. "We did not send her a bag of flour after harvest, so she has made a winter spell."

"No," said Bran. "This is no spell. It's just a long winter. No more than that."

But no one listened to Bran. He was not a village man. He had come from far off and then he had married Edith.

Like all the village women, Edith had dark hair and brown eyes. But Edmund their son was like Bran. His hair was as gold as the sun and his eyes were green like grass.

20

As well as looking strange, Bran did strange things.
His hut was up on Wookey Hill, above the village.
The Witch could toss rocks down on it!
So far she had not, but she could at any time.

Then of all things, Bran dug a well. Edith did not
have to go to the river for water now, but Bran and
Edmund had a long walk to the fields. Silly Bran.
What could a stranger like him know about
their Wild Witch?

But before long the winter was over. The snow
melted. Mud was everywhere. Water rushed down
the hill, and one morning the river ran over
its banks. All the village huts were flooded,
but not Bran's house on the hill.

Later that morning Edmund went up the hill to look
at the village. He did not go as far as Wookey Hole,
but he did look up at the cave. It was a big
black hole in the rocks and it went deep into
the hill.

"The Witch must have eyes as good as a cat's,"
Edmund thought.

Just then thin arms grabbed him in a tight hug and someone shook him and shook him. Then he saw a thin old face close to his. It had a long red nose and a pointed chin. Hair like old wool fell on his face and there was a terrible smell of old rags, rats and other things. This must be the Witch of Wookey.

"Do not come to my cave, Green Eyes," she cackled like a mad old hen. "Go away, little frog! Go!"

She gave Edmund a push so that he fell down the hill, then he ran and ran. Her mad laugh rang out over the hill after him, but when he looked back she was not there. "I will never go near her cave again," he said. "Never!"

Sad to say the spell was still at work in
the village. Day after day something happened and
the Witch was blamed. A hut fell in the river.
Sheep ran off. Pigs got out. Hens did not lay.
Cows gave no milk. Crops came up green and then died.
The goats were sick. Then . . . then . . .
the children were sick, very sick. But not Edmund.
Why was that?

Bran said it was because the river water was bad.

"No. It is Wookey Witch and her spell," said the
villagers. "What does Bran know about that Wild One?"
they asked.

The villagers went up the hill to ask the Witch to
take her spell away. They left gifts, but no one
saw her. Just her mad laugh rang out from the cave.
Edmund could hear it when he went to bed at night.
He made up his mind to help the children.

He went up to the cave. He felt very alone and
not at all brave. "Hello!" he shouted, but it was
more like a squeak. "Hello!"

He smelt the Witch before he saw her. She came out
of the dark cave and hissed.

"So it is you Green Eyes," she said.

Edmund's legs shook. "Can you help the children?"
he said. "They are very sick."

"I help no one, little frog. No one helps me.
Tell them that in the village," she said, then
she was gone.

Sadly Edmund went home and found the house full of village men. They had come to ask Bran to go to see the Bishop in the city of Wells. No one from the village had been to Wells, but Bran had come from far off. He would know the way and what to say to the Bishop. Then the Bishop would get rid of the Witch and her spell.

"The children are sick from the river water," said Bran. "Take the water from our well."

Just the same Bran did go to Wells. So did Edmund and some of the village men. It was a very long walk and at last they came to the city. Edmund thought the houses were as tall as trees and the cathedral seemed to go right up into the sky!

A cross man at the gate of the cathedral saw Bran and the villagers.

"Be off, you lot!" he said. "The Bishop has no time for you." He shut the gate and would not let them go on.

"What can we do now?" Edmund asked.

"We will wait," said Bran. "The Bishop must come by at some time."

So they sat down by the gate. They ate some food and waited. The sun went down and still they waited.

At last Edmund heard horses in the street, and there was the Bishop. He looked splendid in his red robes, with gold rings on his fingers.

Everyone pushed to be near the Bishop, so Edmund did not hear all that was said to him. Suddenly the Bishop clapped his hands. "I will not go to Wookey," he said. "Bring your Witch to me."

"We can't catch that Wild One," said someone.

"What rot!" said the Bishop. "I will not go to Wookey."

"But who will help the sick children?" Edmund cried out. Then he felt the Bishop's eyes on him.

"Someone will go to help, little boy," said the Bishop. No more was said and the Bishop went on to the cathedral.

So they waited again and after a long time, a thin little monk came to them. He had a flask of holy water in his hand. He looked so small and young they wondered what he could do to help with the Wild Witch.

But the next day they all went to Wookey and the monk went up the hill to the cave. All the villagers came up behind him and Edmund went too.

He saw the Witch hop off into her cave. He saw the thin little monk stop and stand still. The monk looked into the dark cave and listened. Then he ran into the cave after the Witch.

The little monk could not see the Witch, but he could hear her. Her mad laugh was all round him.

"Stop!" he shouted. "Stop!"

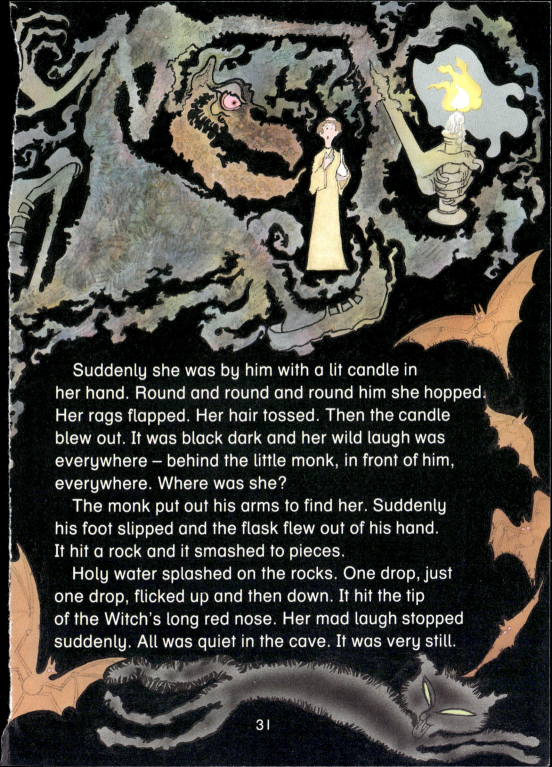

Suddenly she was by him with a lit candle in
her hand. Round and round and round him she hopped.
Her rags flapped. Her hair tossed. Then the candle
blew out. It was black dark and her wild laugh was
everywhere – behind the little monk, in front of him,
everywhere. Where was she?

The monk put out his arms to find her. Suddenly
his foot slipped and the flask flew out of his hand.
It hit a rock and it smashed to pieces.

Holy water splashed on the rocks. One drop, just
one drop, flicked up and then down. It hit the tip
of the Witch's long red nose. Her mad laugh stopped
suddenly. All was quiet in the cave. It was very still.

All the villagers rushed into the cave. Edmund ran in too. Someone lit a torch. They found the thin little monk. They found the Witch too. They found she had turned to stone.

The Wild One had gone, but that is not the end of the story. Soon huts were built on the hill, away from the river. The villagers dug wells for water and the children did not get sick in the same way again.

No one went up to Wookey Hole for a long, long time, but **you** can go there. A big stone like a witch is there still for you to see.